Feeding the Bears

Doug Humes

©2012

Feeding the Bears

It was time for afternoon cookies and the bears had gathered at the edge of the forest. Baby Bear and Momma Bear were there, plus three or four others whose names I've forgotten. My mother and her live-in caregiver, Dick, knew them well, having been camping for a couple of months in their RV on Dick's five acres of Idaho wilderness. I was there for a quick visit to check on Mom's condition and to find out more about Dick, her recently-hired companion.

Mom's decision to hire him six months ago had surprised my brothers and me since she hadn't mentioned she was looking for a caregiver. But I wasn't surprised she'd hooked up with a younger man and gone adventure-traveling; she'd done this before. Practical and business-minded, I figured she'd given plenty of thought to her decision. But now she was 85 and frail, and my brothers and I were keeping a closer watch.

In honor of my visit, they wanted to show me how they fed the bears. We were sitting in folding lawn chairs next to the RV which was parked in the cool shade so Mom could be as comfortable as possible. The black bears, anticipating 'cookie time', were about fifty feet away and looking intently in our direction. I was reassured by Mom and Dick's calm demeanor; they acted as if this were no different than feeding squirrels at the park. I admired Mom's adventurous spirit and courage to push her abilities despite her age, so I sat and watched, nervous but fascinated, trying to look relaxed. I didn't approve of feeding wildlife, particularly bears, but I was a guest and kept my mouth shut.

The routine was to throw several dozen cookies along the edge of the forest and loudly crumple the empty plastic cartons to get the bears' attention. While most of them ate their cookies close to the woods, Dick slowly lured 'Baby Bear' toward us, tossing cookies ever closer. Hands crippled with arthritis, Mom needed Dick's help wedging a cookie between her gnarled fingers, and too weak to hold out her arm, had to rest it on his knee. She leaned forward, eyes wide with excitement, urging the small bear closer with cooing words of encouragement, just like a kid at the Petting Zoo. The brave bear crawled toward Mom, with neck outstretched, nose and ears twitching. Now just a foot away, he slowly raised-up on his front legs and used his lips to gently pull the cookie from her fingers.

Thankfully, one hand-fed cookie was enough, and Dick stood up and shooed the bears away. Mom had a big grin on her face and watched affectionately as the bears disappeared into the forest. Dick was pleased and he and Mom talked fondly of Baby Bear's performance. I tried to look appreciative of their bear training skills, but I thought they were being foolish. There were so many questionable things about Mom's situation, and feeding the bears, no doubt illegal, was just one more cause for concern.

Should my brothers and I allow Mom to live this way? Was wilderness camping too risky for a frail 85 year-old? What should we think of her hired companion who had no training as a caregiver? If she was legally competent to vote, sign contracts, manage her money, and drive, surely she could manage her health care. Society might consider her decisions more foolish than wise, but exactly what are the rules in this case, and who was I to judge? I had rejected family and society's expectations most of my life; I wasn't about to deny anyone their dreams. Besides, she wasn't complaining – she was happy! She talked excitedly of the places they had seen on their RV adventures, and I could tell by the tone of her voice she liked having Dick in her life. Nevertheless, my brothers and I would have preferred she move into an assisted-living facility where she would get professional care, and feeding the bears wouldn't be allowed.

They invited me to give up my motel room and move out to the property with them. Dick said I could sleep in the old school bus that he lived in before Mom and the RV came into his life. He said it was a bit of a mess though; a bear had broken in through the rear door window and "trashed the place" while they were away earlier in the summer. I could see a mattress protruding from the rear door window, preventing further intrusions, I guessed. I didn't even look inside, nor did I inspect the nearby crudely constructed outhouse. I wasn't prepared for camping in these conditions, and I didn't enjoy their company. They were both talkative, opinionated and up-tight; a good match for each other, but not for me.

My relationship with Mom was distant but respectful. The child-mother bonds from my infancy didn't survive my unhappy, rebellious teenage years. She became the disciplinarian in the family and made my life miserable trying to give me the education and social skills she thought necessary for success. My interest in drums was rejected in favor of uninspiring piano lessons, and when I was finally allowed to quit, she guilt-tripped me by saying: "I'm so sorry you're quitting - you were just getting good." It was assumed that my brother and I would go to college, so she pressured us to get good grades at the expense of friends and fun. Neither she nor my father seemed to have any emotional understanding of my misery and resentment, and while my father withdrew from family life, Mom overcompensated. Dinner time showcased our family dysfunction: Mom, having grown up with lively meal time arguments and discussions with her brothers, challenged us with questions, trying to start a conversation. "Russ, Andy, Doug, tell us what you did today." I could sense her frustration with my father who didn't like to talk about his work, preferred to eat silently and quickly, escaping to the kitchen to wash dishes as soon as possible. I felt like we were being tested, and years later the sound of her voice at dinner time still gave me stomach cramps. When I got through college, moved out of the house and was on my own, it became easier to see that my parents were basically good people, just lacking parenting skills and the ability to deal with their emotions. Nevertheless, I avoided my parents, never able to rid myself of the negative associations I had developed in my youth.

After two days of visiting, I was ready to head home. I had done my filial duty. Mom was happy and had someone to look after her, and I was happy to have someone other than me assume that responsibility. I had to get back to work and said we would visit again in a month when they stopped by my place in western Washington on their way to Florida.

Born to be Wild

Mom had grown up on a farm in upstate New York but left the nest for college in Ohio and then Colorado, where she met my father. When he returned from WWII and they married, she was excited to move to New York City where he worked as a lawyer for General Motors. She wanted to be an airline stewardess and travel, but Dad said no, and within a few years they had moved to the suburbs and my older brother Andy was born and a year later, me. Dad liked his routine and wasn't a risk-taker like Mom, so she had to find adventures close to home. Raising two sons with an emotionally detached husband wasn't challenging enough, so she took part time jobs with the elementary school, the PTA, and the Republican Party. Later, while I was getting into trouble in Junior High School, she was commuting into the City, studying to get a Masters Degree in History as a set up for teaching. She taught for a year or two before getting unexpectedly pregnant, and once again she was tied down to raising a child, my brother Greg, 14 years younger than me. When she turned 50, she became a part time travel agent and arranged a trip to South East Asia to visit me in the Peace Corps. A few years later, Dad, 13 years older than Mom, was ready to retire to Florida. Mom tried it for a few years but was concerned with the poor quality of the public school Greg was attending. I suspect there was more to it than that; I don't think she was ready for the retired life, especially if Dad didn't want to travel.

She took Greg north to the small town in New York where she had grown up, and sold real estate with her brother. Dad wouldn't support her or Greg, but the real estate market was good and she made money. When Dad contracted Lou Gehrig's disease, she and Greg moved back to Florida to take care of him. After he died and Greg left for college in Seattle, she moved to Amarillo, Texas to learn investing from a long-time friend. After a few years, it was back to Florida where, now in her early 60's, she hooked up with a younger man and, just for fun, they drove to Costa Rica and back, encountering burglars and major car repairs along the way.

I appreciated her unsettled ways, myself having gone from the Peace Corps to a hippy commune, to a series of odd jobs including commercial fishing and furniture making, then Grad School, fisheries consulting in Alaska, and finally two years working for politicians in Washington, DC and Alaska. When that path came to a dead end, I turned to boats, got a Captain's License and worked on the waters of Puget

Sound. We kept in touch with phone calls, letters, and yearly visits, and while we shared an adventurous spirit, that was all we had in common. We got along, but we didn't hang-out.

After the trip to Costa Rica and the end of that relationship, she found a retirement community with lots of friendly neighbors. She had about twenty good years there, including a short marriage until her husband's death from alcohol. She kept traveling, spending summers in the North East managing two rental properties, and making occasional trips to Washington State to see Greg and me.

As the years went by, her strength declined, she started falling, and her driving was getting dangerous. Greg and wife Elise invited Mom to move in with them. It was a pretty good deal: They owned a house with an available room; they both had experience caring for the elderly from their years working at a nursing home, and Elise had gone on to become a nurse. As an extra bonus, they had two kids, Mom's only grandchildren. A more family-oriented grandmother might have accepted the offer, but Mom was not inclined that way. She said Seattle was too cold, damp and bad for her arthritis.

Andy and I couldn't come close to Greg's offer so there was never a discussion about moving in with us. Luckily for me, Mom wasn't interested in sharing a house. She had grown more independent-minded over the years and for her, quality-of-life meant staying in her own home with her routines, her pets and her stuff. And that was fine with us as long as she was safe, but that was no longer the case. We encouraged her to explore the idea of 'assisted living', but she wasn't interested.

It wasn't her nature to discuss her plans or ask our advice, let alone share her fears or desires. She let her actions speak for her. So when she put the bumper sticker on her otherwise sticker-less station wagon a few years after she moved to the retirement community, I read it as an ominous forewarning: *Get Even - Live Long Enough to Become a Problem for Your Children*. It was funny while she was in good health and it fit in with the other neighborhood bumper stickers, like *I'm Spending my Children's Inheritance*. I would have preferred that one; I wasn't counting on any inheritance, and I most definitely did not want her to become a problem-parent. But by the time she turned 85 and was losing her ability to live alone, ...*Problem for Your Children* was losing its humor.

The Road Less Traveled

Mom had come to a fork in the road. The right turn, down the well-traveled path, would take her to an assisted-living facility, then a nursing home, and finally to the crematorium. She had a good idea what was down that road, having spent several weeks in a nursing home recovering from a fall. And she had watched her retirement-community neighbors, one by one, giving up their house, car, and most of their stuff for a room in 'assisted living'. She rebelled. The left fork was not clear at all, but she was adventurous, stubborn, and always ready to fight for what she believed, and now she was fighting for her independence. But she knew she couldn't do it alone. As luck would have it, one autumn day, Dick knocked on the front door of Mom's double-wide manufactured home. He was down from Idaho for the winter, staying with his elderly father a few blocks away, looking for work, and wondering if Mom wanted her house painted. He was the answer to her prayers.

Over the course of our weekly phone calls with Mom, my brothers and I were startled to learn she had hired Dick to paint the house and help with chores. He was also moving into the guest room, and they were buying a used RV and planning on driving to Idaho for the summer. She sent us a photocopy of his driver's license; he was sixty years old, 6 feet tall, about 200 lbs and had a nice smile. Her only explanation: "I am paying Dick to care for me," written across the top of the page. It seemed rushed, but it eased our concerns about her living alone.

Problems for the Children

Andy lived a couple of hours away from Mom and was the first of us to visit and report: Dick seemed friendly and very attentive toward Mom. Three months later Greg flew to Florida for a week-long visit and discovered his favorite ivory chess set and some old Persian rugs were missing. Neither Dick nor Mom was concerned, suggesting they would turn up eventually. Dick had also started organizing all her financial papers and most surprising of all, he had moved out of the back guest room and was now sleeping with her. When Greg asked Dick a few probing questions, Dick got hostile and wouldn't speak to Greg for the rest of the visit. Mom was sorry that Greg didn't get along with Dick, but seemed to accept that this would be a consequence of her decision to hire him. I called Mom's lawyer to get his reaction to Mom's new situation, but only got confirmation that it was weird but legal.

If there was ever a time to try to explain her thoughts and feelings so my brothers and I could understand what was going on, now would have been the time, but those kinds of communication bridges had never been built. She didn't seem to have the emotional skills for those kinds of discussions nor did I. When she told me, after Greg's visit, that "It's okay to visit as long as you don't give me any advice or tell me what to do", I gave up hope of an enlightening conversation.

If an explanation was needed, Dick had one, no matter how ridiculous. According to him, he was doing us a service by throwing out a lot of Mom's 'worthless junk'. When the antique ship's bell clock disappeared – a family heirloom that had been a wedding gift to her mother and father - he talked about it as if it was a cheap thrift store clock: 'It didn't keep accurate time ... it was noisy... you had to keep winding it up...it was collecting dust...no one was expressing any interest in it'. Knowing that he used his earnings to buy rare coins, stamps and gems, and seemed to know the value of all Mom's jewelry, I suspected he had sold the clock to an antique dealer or pawn shop. I suggested that in the case of antique heirlooms, he consult Mom first before removing them, and rather than throw them in the garbage he should sell them and give the money to Mom. I asked Mom if she wanted me to get more involved, especially since it was her who alerted me to the clock's disappearance. "No" she said. "I'll deal with Dick when I get more energy". She never did, and Dick efficiently got rid of most of her stuff, including a packed storage unit. I didn't care about the stuff, but I was bothered that Dick appeared to be stealing. I asked her lawyer about this and was told it could be explained as 'poor judgment' and would be difficult to prove.

Dick said he was sleeping with Mom for "safety reasons". This way he could help her to the bathroom at night. As Dick tells it, one night shortly after he moved into the back guest room, Mom fell and blocked her bedroom door, making it difficult for him to get in and help. Their plan for avoiding future emergencies was for Dick to sleep in bed with Mom. I found this weird because of their age difference, but part of their 'Deal' was a private relationship that they didn't feel the need to elaborate, and I didn't want to know.

Mom's money was no doubt a central part of the 'Deal'. She apparently had plenty, he didn't have enough, and they seemed to have agreed on a slow transfer to Dick as long as he took care of her. After she told Greg privately that she "had him right where she wanted him", I speculated that her employment strategy was to keep Dick on a 'short leash' by paying him in cash once a week, with pay-raises as her health deteriorated.

When the financial system started breaking down in 2007, it probably wasn't hard for Dick to convince Mom to start 'cashing-out' her accounts and stash the money in a large safe he installed in the house. They shared a fear of stock market crashes and failed banks, and she must have worried that Dick might not stick around if she ran out of money. She had always been a careful manager of her accounts and investments, so bank staff naturally became suspicious when she started closing accounts, paying penalties, and withdrawing large amounts of cash. "We know your mother", they told me, "and this isn't like her." By this time Mom's voice was weak and Dick was more than willing to take control of the conversation and speak for her. Considering he wasn't related, wasn't a professional caregiver, and the twenty-five year age difference, the bank felt obligated to alert my brothers and me as well as the Elder Abuse agency to the possibility that Mom was being scammed.

Based on our recent visits and phone conversations with her, my brothers and I were pretty sure Mom was still competent to be making financial decisions, and soon we had confirmation. The bank staff would take Mom aside and ask her questions, and the Elder Abuse staff would visit Mom at home. They interviewed my brothers and me as well. She didn't like this meddling and would give terse, sarcastic answers like "I don't trust the banks", or "I need to buy a new refrigerator". She might be making questionable decisions, but she seemed to know what she was doing. Even though we suspected Dick was manipulating her, unless we wanted to try to prove her incompetence by applying for guardianship and taking her to court (and there was no consensus among my brothers for that drastic action) there wasn't much we could do.

Despite their disturbing behavior, we could see that her life was transformed in a very positive way. She had not only found someone who could help her stay out of the dreaded nursing home, but had also found a companion who shared her corny sense of humor, would argue politics, was someone to tease and who called her Sweetie. She was excited to have a partner who shared her enjoyment of travel and adventure and was looking forward to their upcoming RV trips. It was also obvious that she didn't want interference from her family and was placing her complete trust in her new man. She reminded me of my behavior when I was in my twenties - separating from family and paying little heed to consequences. 'Not much difference between young and foolish, and old and foolish' I thought to myself.

The Gun Totin', Pot Smokin', Vegetable eatin', Gigolo

They were an odd couple, and the details of their relationship made for interesting stories when I'd meet with friends. Most were astonished and certain Mom was being preyed upon. I often had to defend her and argue she knew what she was doing, she was tough, and this was her best option. I felt my brothers and I had been diligent by doing a background check on Dick, contacting Elder Abuse agencies, requesting 'wellness checks' by the local sheriff, and reviewing the situation with her lawyer. We even offered to help her find a different caregiver. "No", she would say. "I need Dick!" After hearing many stories, one friend summed up Dick as a 'gun totin', pot smokin', vegetable eatin', gigolo'.

Shortly after he started working for Mom, they went to a gun show and Dick bought a .45 semi-automatic hand gun. She was okay with guns, and liked the idea of having 'protection' in case of threatening situations. And once they started hoarding cash at the house, they no doubt worried about burglars. One day Dick was napping on the living room couch, his new .45 close at hand, when a gust of wind caused the window curtains to flap noisily. Dick was startled and bolted to a sitting position with the gun pointed out the window. Recounting the story, Mom casually said, "I told him 'Don't shoot till you see the whites of their eyes'". She thought it was funny! I give him credit for making Mom feel safe and not accidently shooting anyone.

He admitted to smoking marijuana and it seemed to keep him functioning in his 24/7, 365 days-a-year-job for which he had no background or training. Mom was a whiskey drinker, but accepted Dick's marijuana habit once it was obvious that it made life easier for both of them. When Dick told me about rolling a joint and getting 'stoned' before driving the RV down one of his favorite scenic highways, Mom leaned over and gave him a good-natured slap on the knee saying: "Yup, and he hasn't hit anything yet!"

Gigolo wasn't quite the right term, but it was close. Even though he stuck with her for six years, his dedication was based more on greed than compassion. His weekly salary started out at $500 and by year six was up to $1500. Mom knew this was the cost of a live-in caregiver so she didn't mind the expense, and she had the money. But in the end, $78,000 a year, tax free, plus room and board, wasn't enough for Dick, and he protested to the end that Mom still owed him more.

Most would say that Dick was a poor choice for a caregiver, but not Mom. From her point of view, he was a winner; he was a good companion, made it possible to live at home, and provided travel and adventure. He wasn't perfect, but by now she was used to imperfect relationships and put up with his behavior without complaint. "I need Dick!" was her reaction to any suggestion that he was a problem. End of discussion.

It Gets Worse

At the end of their second summer in Idaho, Mom fell and fractured two neck vertebrae. She spent six weeks recuperating in a nursing home, Dick lived in the RV at the nursing home parking lot, and Greg and I made several visits. When she was well enough to travel, they flew back to Florida leaving the RV on Dick's property. We all thought her traveling days were over, but the next year they flew back for one last Idaho summer. After that Mom was too frail for the long trip and they stayed in Florida for the next year and a half.

It was at that point Dick began acting stranger than usual. During one of my weekly phone conversations with Dick and Mom, he announced that he had started rewriting her Will. "It's too long" he said. "I think I can say what needs to be said in one page." Mom said she was ready to talk with her lawyer, but Dick was balking. My offer to help was declined. Dick must have realized his attempt to rewrite the Will could get messy if Mom's lawyer and my brothers and I got involved, so he dropped that plan after a few weeks. I wasn't too concerned about the Will. I figured Mom and her lawyer could deal with it, and I'd get involved only as a last resort.

Dick started keeping the house too hot in the summer and too cold in the winter. The police, who we called regularly for surprise "wellness checks", would find the house remarkably hot in the summertime. And on one of my visits, on a winter morning, I found Mom bundled up in blankets inside the cold house. When I asked why he didn't turn on the heat, Dick started opening windows, explaining: "It's warming up outside and the breeze will soon heat the house, and it's a lot cheaper than running the inefficient heater." I thought this was much too stressful for an elder, not to mention a ridiculous explanation, so I had Mom's doctor send her and Dick a letter recommending keeping the house temperature between 70 and 80 degrees year 'round. When I questioned her about her comfort, she would always say: "Everything's fine. No need to do anything." She couldn't reach the thermostat anyway, and had given up arguing with Dick.

For years she'd had problems swallowing due to a mild stroke. The result was a lot of coughing at meal time and probably some aspiration of food into her lungs. She didn't like the recommended thickened liquids and Dick was willing to ignore the doctors as well. Sometimes he'd be feeding her when I'd call, and her coughing would make conversation impossible. In the depths of my most pessimistic thoughts, I wondered if he was subconsciously trying to kill her by inducing stress and pneumonia.

Her complacency was frustrating but not difficult to understand. Greg speculated, and I agreed that this was like the Stockholm Syndrome, where the captive eventually comes to believe her captor is her only chance for survival and becomes completely dependent. There was no doubt in my mind she believed Dick was the only person between her and the nursing home. I saw her as a willing participant in a dysfunctional, abusive relationship. What's worse, I wondered, a bad relationship or isolation in a nursing home? It was maddening to think that this was the better of two options. The consensus among my brothers and I was that this was the price she was willing to pay to stay out of the nursing home. She still appeared competent, didn't appear to be suffering, wasn't complaining, and was unwavering in her aversion to interference from her sons. None of us was ready to disrupt our lives to intervene in what would likely be a hostile situation, so we kept in touch and waited.

In the early summer of her 89th year, her voice became so weak that I could hardly understand her over the phone. I had an intuition there might not be many more opportunities for conversation, so I decided to fly to Florida so we could talk more easily. I didn't know what we would talk about, but it seemed like the right thing to do. Not wanting to alarm Mom with my concern, I used the excuse that I wanted to celebrate her July birthday, and that I would try to get Greg to come along. He hadn't been to Florida since the altercation with Dick five years ago and never expected to go back, but I reasoned with him that she was losing her voice and this might be the last time she would be strong enough for a conversation. Andy could meet us and we'd have a party.

As soon as Greg figured out a date when he could travel, I called to let Mom and Dick know when we would arrive. A couple of days later I called to prod Dick about maintaining the air conditioning and was alarmed to find the phone disconnected, "at the request of the occupant", the telephone company said. In a panic, I called the sheriff's department. They were soon at Mom's house and reported it empty and the car gone. They learned that Dick had told a neighbor they were heading for the Appalachian Mountains to escape the Florida heat. When we called Dick's father to find out what he knew of the situation, we learned Dick had called to report they were doing fine, heading north, staying in motels, and he would soon write to us and explain.

Missing Persons

Shit! How could they go on an unannounced vacation when he knew my brothers and I were coming to visit? Why didn't Mom say something when we were on the phone just days before? What would cause Dick to take such drastic action?

After two weeks with no word from Dick, Andy filed a Missing Persons report and within 10 days the sheriff had tracked her arthritis medication shipments to a small town in southwest North Carolina. The local sheriff paid them a visit and reported no signs of abuse, and that Mom was doing well and 'Just wants to be left alone.' The local Department of Children and Families also started visiting after suspicious banking activity. They opened a Case Report on Mom, interviewed my brothers and me, and we stayed in regular communication over the next two months. They never found any signs of coercion and reported that Mom appeared competent.

If it took several interviews for Mom and Dick to seem legitimate, they often didn't pass the 'first impression' test, so it wasn't surprising that North Carolina banks would be suspicious. I'd seen the routine at their Florida bank: Mom would sit quietly hunched over in the wheel chair, bundled up to stay warm, wearing huge dark sunglasses to cut the glare; Dick would explain what transactions Mom wanted executed; the teller would ask Mom if that was correct; Mom would weakly say 'yes'; Dick would help her sign the order, and then collect the cash. Dick's assertive, brusque, controlling behavior and his caregiver status no doubt raised 'red flags' at the bank, and would cause them to question Mom's competency.

A year later, as we prepared for the guardianship hearing, we learned they had failed another 'first impression' test when a North Carolina county clerk denied Dick a marriage license. Dick had appeared at the clerk's desk alone while Mom remained in the car. The clerk, perhaps suspicious of the age difference and the absence of the bride, insisted on walking to the car to see her. She later told me "I took one look at her eyes and I could tell she was in no condition to get married. I didn't think she could even hold a pen."

My brothers and I made no plans to fly to North Carolina. As long as she was appearing competent to the Elder Abuse social worker and not objecting to her living situation, we weren't about to disrupt our lives and begin a court battle against Dick and Mom where the outcome was uncertain. We had gotten used to their dysfunctional relationship and her turning away from us. We had given up on the idea of her moving in with one of us; we had given up promoting assisted living; we had given up trying to be helpful. I didn't even want to visit.

We sent cards and letters instead, hoping they would elicit a call and an explanation. They never called, but we did get a response from Dick. He started sending us nasty cards and letters, sometimes written in shaky handwriting, impersonating Mom, or sometimes writing for himself. The message was always the same: "Leave us alone". He accused us of "criminal harassment" for instigating visits from the sheriff and social services. He threatened "protection orders and criminal charges". In his mind our motivation was clear: we weren't grateful or satisfied with Mom's previous monetary gifts and now we wanted more. "She is giving all her money to charity. There is none left for you." His illustrated sign-off: "Grow up. Get a Job. Leave your poor mother alone. Fuck You and Good Bye." At the bottom of the page was his simple line drawing of a fist with the middle finger raised. p.s., "Stop calling the police."

His letters were disturbing and revealed an anger I hadn't seen before. The only plausible explanation was that Dick believed my brothers and I were about to begin legal action and would take control of Mom's affairs, at which point he'd be out of a job. He most likely told her we were coming to separate them and put her in a nursing home. To them, disappearing must have seemed like the only way to maintain their relationship. In reality, my brothers and I were worried he would abandon her. If she wanted Dick, we weren't going to get in her way.

At the end of the summer they left the mountains of North Carolina telling the social worker they were heading south for the winter. We assumed they would return to Mom's Florida house, but when they didn't turn up, we filed a second Missing Person's report. Once again we found them by tracing her medication, this time in southern Georgia. We resumed our requests for 'wellness checks' by the sheriff, and continued sending cards and letters. Once again, the sheriff would find Mom aware, rested, safe, and relatively healthy - and repeating her mantra, "I don't want to go to a nursing home. I just want to be left alone." At the beginning of the hot summer, they disappeared once more.

Train Wreck

In early September I drove to eastern Washington to spend Labor Day weekend with friends. I arrived Thursday afternoon and no sooner settled in when a call from Greg jolted me. He'd received an email from a nurse in north Georgia looking for relatives of an elderly woman admitted to the hospital under suspicious circumstances. Mom! "If you are related, please call immediately. Family support at this time would be greatly appreciated". Shit! Mom in dire straits, thousands of miles away, and my brothers and I having to intervene with little time to prepare. At least we knew where she was and that she was safe.

It quickly became obvious that I, unemployed and with few commitments, would be the one flying to Georgia. I accepted this responsibility but I was resentful. I had been struggling for the past three years to start an inspiring, innovative educational program and I was trying to focus all my energy in that direction. Now I feared I would be caught up in a hostile, confrontational situation. Any love or compassion I had for my mother had been worn thin by her rejection of my attempts to intervene over the past two years. Now, like the bumper sticker said, she was just a problem for her children.

I spent Friday getting focused, collecting information, making travel arrangements, and coordinating with my brothers. Gabriel, the nurse who had contacted my brother, told me Mom was not dying, but having medical issues related to the aspiration of food and liquids into her lungs. I learned that when Dick had taken Mom to the local clinic earlier that week, the doctor became suspicious. Dick claimed the pizza he was feeding her wasn't a problem, but the doctor thought otherwise. He also suspected dementia. He recommended Mom be admitted to the hospital, but Dick declined and they returned to their rental house. The next day Gabriel visited Mom and also became concerned with Dick's feeding practices. The doctor ordered Dick to take Mom to the emergency room and threatened to send an ambulance if he didn't act immediately. Mom was admitted, and the nurse began searching for relatives.

Up until now it had been either 'Mom's disappeared! What do we do?' or 'We've found Mom! What do we do?' This time was different: Mom no longer passed the competency test and she would be held in the hospital for observation over Labor Day weekend, giving relatives time to respond. I accepted my fate; all I had to do was drive home, pack a bag, and get to the airport.

Rescue

I arrived at the Atlanta airport Sunday morning, rented a car and headed for the rolling hills of the Appalachian Mountains. At the recommendation of Gabriel, I checked into a motel 15 miles from the hospital. She told me to stay out of town until I had guardianship papers, fearing Dick would see me, know something was up, and disappear with Mom. Monday was the Labor Day holiday and gave me a chance to rest and adjust to my new situation. First impressions were good: friendly and helpful people, perfect weather, comforting food.

There was no relaxing on Tuesday. By mid afternoon I had met with Gabriel, found a lawyer, gone before the judge, and had Emergency Guardianship papers in hand. With heart pounding, I went to the hospital to find Mom and fire Dick. At the suggestion of my lawyer, I requested a Civil Standby, and two deputy sheriffs met me at the hospital parking lot. With them by my side, we went to Mom's room, knocked on the door and invited a surprised Dick into the hallway. "I'm now Mom's guardian" I said. "If you have objections, you should attend the hearing on Friday. Now I'd like you to leave the hospital and not return." I was nervous, expecting a belligerent response after the threatening letters he had sent during the past 14 months. My worries were for nothing. The presence of the deputies left him speechless. Mom must have heard us in the hall and started calling Dick's name. "Hear that?" he said. "She needs me. I can't leave her." "I'm taking care of her now" I said. He looked at the deputies once more and said "Well, this is a surprise! Okay, let me get my things out of the room." It took just minutes.

One of the deputies suggested we retrieve Mom's things from the rental house, but before we left, I dashed into her room. She looked bad: oxygen tubes in her nose, a feeding tube down her throat, an IV drip stuck in her skinny arm, and a startled look in her eyes. I told her I was here to take care of her and I'd be right back. She didn't respond, and I'm not sure she knew who I was, but I knew she was safe.

At the rental house, it didn't take Dick long to empty dresser drawers of Mom's clothing and medication into a couple of suitcases. After all the drama of the last 14 months, to suddenly be watching Dick calmly packing her suitcases was completely out of character with the angry, paranoid and devious person I now believed him to be. The deputy couldn't linger and I didn't want to be alone with Dick, so I left not thinking to ask for Mom's legal, financial, and medical records. It didn't matter at that point. I just wanted to get away from him. As I backed the rental car down the driveway I could see from the corner of my eye his scowling face leaning out the front door. He was furious and thrust his fist at me, middle finger raised.

Back at the hospital, still running on adrenaline, I made calls to my brothers, met with medical staff, and began trying to communicate with Mom. I didn't cry until the next day.

End of the Road

My hopes for having some kind of eleventh hour breakthrough in our relationship were dead. She could barely whisper 'yes' or 'no' or nod her head, her eyes distant, body motionless, vitality gone. She never got better. There would be no end-of-life conversations now; no chance to explain motives, thoughts, fears, hopes; no reconciliation of personalities.

She had always been talkative and I the quiet one; now I was doing all the talking. I told her I was here to take care of her. I lied and said Dick had to go to Florida to be with his sick father. I told her she was in a good place with good medical attention, and that Greg and Andy would be here soon. I used comforting, loving words. I hoped she could hear me and understand. The talking made me feel better. I didn't know what else to do.

Andy and Greg arrived the next day and we met with our lawyer and prepared for the guardianship hearing. On Friday, Dick showed up at the hearing with a lawyer and two witnesses. He defended his record as caregiver, acknowledged he had been denied a marriage license in North Carolina, had gotten Power of Attorney in southern Georgia, and said Mom still owed him money. The doctor said she probably had dementia for months, and a court appointed, neutral observer thought it odd that Dick would expect to be paid to care for the woman he wanted to marry. I said I was ready to assume guardianship responsibilities and would stay as long as she was here.

Early the next week, before the judge handed down the decision, Dick said he would drop his objections to my guardianship with three conditions: He wanted one last visit with Mom; he wanted Mom's manufactured double-wide house in Florida; and he wanted $20,000. I would have granted his first wish, but the staff at the nursing home where Mom was now resting was adamant that Dick not be allowed in and were even locking the doors at night; Dick had apparently sent a hateful note to Mom's doctor after the hearing, calling him a liar and telling him to go to Hell. A few days later, the judge ruled in my favor, Dick turned over Mom's financial papers, and disappeared.

Almost Heaven

By now Greg had returned to work. Andy, self employed, was able to stay another 10 days and help me work through legal, medical, and financial issues. After that, on my own, I slowly settled into what would be a three month vigil.

After a few weeks, I realized it could have been a lot worse; it turned out to be not so bad. I found a motel room that rented by the week, and the one mile walk to and from the nursing home became my favorite part of the day. It was good exercise, and the rural beauty was good for my soul. The small town, population 900, was situated next to a lake, and was connected to the other small Appalachian towns by a two lane highway that snaked through the valleys. It was just the right size. It had everything I needed and I could walk from one end of town to the other. I felt settled.

The nursing home, situated half way up the mountain side, provided some of the best views. From the parking lot I could watch the clouds, feel the warm autumn breezes and hear the faint hum of traffic. I spent a lot of time there making cell phone calls, trying to stay connected to friends and relatives and the life I had so abruptly left.

I can't imagine a better nursing home; clean, neat, and well maintained. It was staffed by friendly and helpful people who not only provided excellent care for Mom, but helped make my stay as comfortable as possible. I learned their names as fast as I could and cultivated friendships as a way to restore some normalcy to my situation and to break down feelings of isolation. We talked about families, firewood, cars, music, the weather, anything.

The residents weren't as cheerful as the staff, understandably so. Most didn't want to be there. They wanted to be home, able to drive, independent and free. They wanted to be healthy and fit once more. It took some time to get to know them but once I learned their names and we started talking, they quickly became part of the nursing home 'family' that was now my life. I'd sometimes sit in the hall, or the 'front porch' as it was called, and visit with them or play guitar. I needed to be around people, and they were happy to talk.

They were all in better condition than my mother. She was a wretched sight: less than 100 pounds, skin and bones, legs drawn up in the fetal position, breathing slowly, eye lids closed. She was on life support with her feeding tube now plumbed directly into her stomach. Long periods of lying listless would be interrupted by painful muscle contractions causing cries of pain and wide open eyes. Pain relieving morphine would sometimes give her face a possessed look making her almost unrecognizable.

Her communication was limited to occasional faint whispers, a nod of the head, or the signaling movement of her one finger that wasn't frozen with arthritis. Speech therapy was discontinued after a couple of weeks when it was apparent she wasn't responding. She may have been speechless but you could hear her howls of pain in the hallway even with the door closed. She wasn't the only resident vocalizing distressing sounds - some moaned or repeated phrases incessantly - but Mom's howling tortured me.

With Dick now gone and me assuming the guardianship role, feelings of compassion returned. Years of memories crept back into my mind, overcoming the past six years of alienation, reconnecting me with Mom. Our bonds were weak but numerous, and represented the longest relationship I'd ever had. I couldn't help but feel sad for the impending loss of someone who helped shape my life, for better or worse.

The prognosis was not good. She was in stable condition but was never going to get better. She would continue living like this until she either got pneumonia or her heart stopped. With her being in such a tenuous condition, I wanted to spend as much time with her as possible. I made arrangements with the nursing home to have meals in Mom's room, and soon my visits revolved around breakfast, lunch and dinner. It motivated me to get up and get moving in the morning and gave structure to my day. A friend shipped my guitar and I played tunes for my silent mother. I went to the library and checked-out a Spanish vocabulary book. I told her about the weather, the TV news, and anything else I felt like talking about. I hoped she could hear me and was comforted by the sound of my voice. I also kept a journal as a way to make sense of my situation.

Mid morning and mid afternoon breaks were part of my routine and got me outside. The walk back and forth to my motel room or around town always energized me and made the six to eight hours a day at the nursing home tolerable. I also made sure I kept busy dealing with legal and financial issues, making phone calls, and running errands.

While the good weather lasted I didn't mind not having a car, but I was told the coming months would be cold and wet, with occasional snow and ice. I had no idea how long Mom would last, but thought I should plan on being there through the winter. I decided I'd fly home at the end of November, retrieve my car, and drive back to Georgia. Andy flew up from Florida to continue the vigil, and after almost three months, I took a break.

There was no relief. I had just gone to sleep on my first night home when a nurse called to say Mom was dying. For her to die without me seemed incredibly sad. After all the years since my childhood, she was now once again part of my daily life. Now I really wanted to be with her, to give what comfort I could in her last hour. It was 2 AM and I doubted Andy, unable to see well enough for night driving, would be able to get to the nursing home. My only consolation was knowing the loving and caring nursing staff would be there to ease her from this life, and I could do no better than that.

Social Conscience

I haven't enjoyed writing this story. Reliving so much unpleasantness has been a miserable experience. I didn't want to remember how I grew more and more detached from my mother when it could have been a time of reconciliation. I didn't want to remember how I was duped by Dick into believing he loved my mother when he was mainly interested in her money. I didn't want to wonder if it might have turned out better if my brothers and I had intervened earlier.

I'm writing this because many friends said I should write it - I suppose because they, like me, thought it amazing. Hopefully I've been able to expose some of the dilemmas we face as we grow old and lose our ability to live independently. For me, the struggle was between Mom's desire for freedom and society's concern for elder abuse. I relied on my intuition and the counsel of my brothers and friends to weigh the options and act, or not act.

Four days after Mom died I started driving back to Georgia. The only way I could bring this episode in my life to a close was to personally thank the people who had cared for my mother and been so supportive during my three month stay. I also wanted to thank those who had sensed Mom's incompetence, found family and supported legal action. In that community, it was expected that family would be the preferred choice when it came time to care for an elderly parent, and certainly not a caregiver who would separate a parent from her family, or confuse love and money, or who might be preying on the elderly.

In the end, I think Mom played her hand pretty well: She avoided the nursing home until she was completely worn out; had a man in her life, for better or worse, to the end; and had saved enough money to pay for it. She pushed the limits of her own physical endurance as well as the limits of what society would tolerate. Feeding the bears is probably illegal, but when you're running out of time, who cares?

Made in the USA
Charleston, SC
29 May 2013